Spoon & Shrapnel

VERSE & WARTIME RECIPES

Sheema Kalbasi

Daraja Press

Published by
Daraja Press
https://darajapress.com

ISBN: 978-1-998309-37-5 (print)

Book and cover design by Kate McDonnell

Library and Archives Canada Cataloguing in Publication
Title: Spoon and shrapnel : verse and wartime recipes / Sheema
Kalbasi.
Names: Kalbasi, Sheema, author
Identifiers: Canadiana 20240512774 | ISBN 9781998309375
(softcover)
Subjects: LCGFT: Poetry. | LCGFT: Literary cookbooks.
Classification: LCC PS3611.A4324 S66 2024 | DDC 811/.6–dc23

This book is a treasure. Sheema Kalbasi offers an exquisitely nourishing combination of simple, sustaining recipes recalled from her war-ravaged Iranian childhood, along with evocative poems asking essential questions – why so much war? What better tables might we be setting together in our shared world?

— **Naomi Shihab Nye**, poet, writer,
author of *The Tiny Journalist* and *Habibi*

It is impossible to overstate the necessity, vitality, power, and beauty of Sheema Kalbasi's *Spoon and Shrapnel: Verses and Wartime Recipes*. Detailing the constant threat of bombings and the adaptive strategies of families navigating scarcity while under the duress of war in the Middle East, *Spoon and Shrapnel* is an alchemical transformation of the sensory and emotional realities of a wartime childhood into a collection of poems and recipes that is as soulful, lovely, and hearty as the best comfort food.

Providing a nuanced exploration of how communities sustain themselves physically and emotionally in the face of violence, this collection includes recipes constructed from rationed goods or procured through black-market means, recipes created under such duress, they often didn't even have the luxury of names. "War inspired its own creativity, / In the absence and lack of ingredients," Kalbasi tells us, and we see the same extraordinary creativity in her poems—creativity that is humble and accessible but also brilliantly crafted and luminously gorgeous, creativity that could likely only be delivered by someone with the nearly magical ability to arrive in the kitchen with odds and ends and scraps and seemingly discordant ingredients, and with them, make a delicious meal.

I remember once being asked which books I would choose if I was stranded on a desert island and could only have one box of books with me. Now that Kalbasi has written *Spoon and Shrapnel*, I'd like to revise my answer. I'd like to include a new book.

— **Melissa Studdard,** poet, librettist,
and co-host of *Poems You Need*

Refuge

We hid in the mouths of closets,
Under the ribs of stairwells,
Bomb shelters like coffins in waiting.
Some of us surfaced, gasping—
Some, the earth swallowed whole.

Sheema Kalbasi

Preface

This narrative chronicles my journey from conflict to tranquility, traversing regions including the Middle East, South Asia, Europe, and the United States. My formative years were profoundly influenced by experiences in war zones, which indelibly shaped both my identity and creative expression. The specter of war played a pivotal role in my development, and through my poetry, I strive to articulate the haunting memories of a childhood spent amidst relentless bombings. The struggle for basic necessities was pervasive during this tumultuous period; staples such as meat and rice —the foundational elements of Iranian cuisine—were often in short supply.

During the final year of war, I experienced a debilitating loss of mobility for three months. Psychological terror manifested in violent coughs that felt as though they might tear my lungs from my chest. I required assistance even to sit or stand. This period was further complicated by the departure of my father and one of my brothers, leaving my youngest brother and me in the care of our mother until we, too, could leave the country. Amidst this chaos, we clung to hope as we clandestinely fled Tehran in the back of a truck that transported us 900 kilometers to safety. Yet, even in such dire circumstances, the pursuit of food became a daily imperative for survival.

Reflecting on my relationship with food, I am reminded of Audrey Hepburn, who also faced the harsh realities of war in her childhood, raised in the Netherlands during the Nazi occupation. Experiencing scarcity firsthand, Hepburn's culinary creativity and resourcefulness became a foundation of connection, much like my own. Her humanitarian work later emphasized alleviating hunger—a mission I deeply resonate with. In 2019, I was invited as the main speaker at the United Nations' World Food Programme in Rome, Italy, where I spoke about food shortages in regions such as the Middle East and South America.

I am not a trained cook, and here I have written from memory, recalling mostly the simplest foods we ate during wartime. Measurements may not be precise; in fact, this is approximate, as life itself was approximate in the precariousness of surviving war. For me, food transcended sustenance; it became a source of connection and hope. This narrative—and the recipes within it—serves as a testament to resilience and creativity in adversity. I do not adhere to strict measurements; rather, I seek to recall the essence of dishes from my childhood, as memory permits.

I encourage you to trust yourself in everything you do, even when measuring ingredients. As you engage with this narrative, consider: How would you navigate life in a war zone? What meals could you prepare with limited resources?

— Sheema Kalbasi

The Season of Ration

It was the season of ration,
The war, like a sieve, drained the days—
Long lines wound like snakes,
And the cupboards emptied.
Rice, cheese, milk, and meat vanished,
Fruits rotted in memory.
I watched my parents press milk to curd,
Hands trembling in the low-lit kitchen.
Today, they would flaunt their craft
On social media—
The perfect pair, cheese in hand,
Children skittering with cats,
Cats darting underfoot,
While bombs pounded their quiet hunger into dust.

Homemade Cheese

Ingredients:

- 1 liter (4 cups) of whole milk
- 2-3 tablespoons of lemon juice or white vinegar
- A pinch of salt
- Some herbs or spices (my parents did not add anything)

What you will will need:

- A heavy-bottomed pot that does not burn easily
- Cheesecloth or just a clean towel will do
- A colander

Directions:

1. Warm the milk

- Pour the milk into the pot and gently warm it over medium heat.
- Stir every now and then so it does not stick. You want it just about ready to boil, but not quite there. Just look for tiny bubbles at the edges.

2. Add the lemon juice or vinegar

- Once the milk is hot, take it off the stove.
- Slowly stir in lemon juice or vinegar. My parents used vinegar. You will see the milk start to curdle – that is how you know it is working. If it does not curdle right away, add a little more juice and keep stirring.

3. Let the magic happen

- Let the milk sit for about 5-10 minutes. You will see the curds (the solid part) separating from the whey (the liquid).

4. Strain the curds

- Place your cheesecloth inside a colander over a big bowl.
- Carefully pour the curds and whey into the colander. The whey will drain into the bowl, leaving you with the curds. If you want a firmer cheese, tie the cloth up and let it hang for 30 minutes to an hour to drip out more liquid.

5. Season and shape

- Once the curds are drained, you can mix in a little salt, or even some herbs.
- If you are making soft cheese, it is ready to eat. If you want it to be firmer, press the cheesecloth with something heavy for an hour or two until it forms a nice block.

6. Enjoy

- Your cheese is done. Store it in the fridge and try to eat it within 3-4 days.

Vegan Cheese Recipe

Ingredients:

- 1 cup blanched almonds
- Water
- Salt (to taste)
- 1 teaspoon lemon juice (or to taste)

Instructions:

1. **Blend ingredients:** In a blender, combine blanched almonds, a little water, and salt. Blend until smooth.
2. **Add lemon juice:** Add lemon juice and blend again until fully incorporated.
3. **Drain the mixture:** Strain the blended mixture through cheesecloth, allowing the excess water to drain. This will give the cheese a crumbly texture.
4. **Make doogh (Persian drink):** The remaining liquid can be mixed with sparkling water and lemon juice to create a Persian drink called doogh.
5. **Alternate doogh recipe:** You can also make doogh with regular yogurt, sparkling water, and salt. Add a pinch of dried mint for extra flavour.

Note: Doogh may not be to everyone's liking, but most Iranians love it.

Recipes in War

With war came a renovation of our home—
Not a real one, just for safety.
The kitchen became a storage room,
The back of the house,
A makeshift kitchen, where meals became stitches.
It was stifling, claustrophobic,
Rice bags like corpses hanging from the ceiling, suspended
To keep the mice at bay.
The house twisted,
As if doors were leading to tunnels,
Reflecting the double life we lived—
Trying to flee, yet unable to escape.
With every explosion, I felt my father unravel,
A chemist in a war-torn lab,
Crafting recipes of survival,
Cooking meals that lacked names
But there were also those that had names.

There was Kolehjoosh—
Dried onions wept in their sorrow,
Each spoonful a tether to the earth we once claimed as home,
A remembrance of what was lost.
Tarkhineh bubbled in despair,
Fermented wheat rising like the dust of our ruins,
Each breath a reminder,
Each bite a defiance against the silence of the night.
Ashkaneh simmered—
Eggs in a broth of brittle dreams,
Herbs and spices mingled with regret,
Passed down like secrets, unspoken,
The weight of the past clinging to the ladle.

I swore I could taste
The blood of our history, thick as the smoke
That choked the sun and smothered our laughter.
And yet, even in this carnage, we fed,
Against the silence of my father's secrets,
His inventive hands weaving life
From the remnants of a shattered world.

Kolehjoosh

This dish is celebrated for its simplicity and versatility, often made with whatever ingredients are on hand, such as beans or herbs, making it a practical choice for families. Certain ingredients are staples in every Persian home, including dried mint, walnuts, kashk, and turmeric, among other pantry essentials. The dish typically features a base of crushed walnuts, sautéed onions, and a unique ingredient called kashk. Kashk is a fermented dairy product commonly used in Persian and other Middle Eastern cuisines. It is made by draining yogurt, boiling it down to thicken, and sometimes drying it into a powder. Kashk has a tangy, salty flavor reminiscent of sour cream or yogurt but with a more intense taste. During times of electricity outages caused by bombings and rockets tolling through the city, Kolehjoosh, Tarkhineh, and Ashkaneh were three regular dishes for my family amid food shortages.

Ingredients:

- 1 cup walnuts (crushed)
- 1 large onion (finely chopped)
- 3-4 cloves garlic (minced)
- 2 tablespoons dried mint
- 2 cups kashk (if you do not have kashk, yogurt works too)
- 2 tablespoons oil (use whatever you have – vegetable or olive is good)
- 1 teaspoon turmeric
- Salt and pepper to taste
- 1-2 cups water (depending on how thick you like it)
- Optional: a pinch of dried herbs like oregano or thyme if you feel fancy.

Instructions:

1. **Start with the onions:** Heat some oil in a big pot over medium heat. Toss in the onions and let them cook slowly until they turn golden and sweet–this can take 10 minutes or so. Be patient; it is worth it. Then add the garlic and give it another minute or two until it smells wonderful.
2. **Walnuts and turmeric next:** Stir in the crushed walnuts and turmeric. Let them toast a bit in the onion mix so everything gets a nice nutty flavor.
3. **Time for the kashk:** Pour in the kashk and a bit of water. Stir it all together well. Let it come to a simmer, and leave it for about 10-15 minutes, stirring it every so often. It will thicken up nicely.
4. **Mint magic:** Heat a little oil in a small pan and quickly fry the dried mint–just for a few seconds. Do not let it burn. Once it is fragrant, add it to the soup with some salt and pepper.
5. **Serve it up:** Spoon your Kolehjoosh into bowls. If you like, drizzle a bit more kashk or yogurt on top. Serve with bread.

Tarkhineh

This is a traditional Persian soup made with fermented yogurt and a grain mixture, often flavored with herbs and spices. It is a hearty and nutritious dish, especially popular in the colder months. Here is a simple recipe for making Tarkhineh.

Ingredients:

For the Tarkhineh Mixture:

- 1 cup of dried tarkhineh (fermented yogurt and grain mix; if unavailable, you can substitute with yogurt, bulgur wheat, and a bit of vinegar)
- 1 cup plain yogurt
- ½ cup bulgur wheat (fine or coarse)
- 1 tablespoon salt
- 1 teaspoon dried mint
- 1 teaspoon turmeric
- ½ teaspoon black pepper
- Water (enough to create a thick paste)

For the Soup:

- 1 large onion (finely chopped)
- 2-3 tablespoons oil (vegetable or olive oil)
- 4-6 cups water (or broth)
- 1-2 cups of chopped vegetables (any preferred veggies)
- Optional: fresh herbs like curly parsley for garnish

Instructions:

1. **Prepare the Tarkhineh mixture:**
   - In a bowl, combine the dried tarkhineh, yogurt, bulgur wheat, salt, dried mint, turmeric, and black pepper.
   - **Gradually add water** until it forms a thick paste. Let it sit for about 30 minutes to allow the flavors to meld.

2. **Sauté the onions:**
   - In a large pot, heat the oil over medium heat. Add the chopped onion and sauté until golden brown and caramelized.
3. **Add water and vegetables:**
   - Pour in the water (or broth) and bring it to a gentle boil.
   - Add the chopped vegetables and cook until they begin to soften (about 10-15 minutes).
4. **Incorporate the Tarkhineh mixture:**
   - Gradually add the Tarkhineh mixture to the pot, stirring well to combine.
   - Reduce the heat and let it simmer for about 20-30 minutes, stirring occasionally. If the soup is too thick, you can add more water to reach your desired consistency.
5. **Serve:**
   - Once the soup has thickened and the flavors have developed, taste and adjust the seasoning if necessary.
   - Ladle the Tarkhineh into bowls and garnish with fresh herbs if desired.

Ashkaneh

This is a traditional Iranian soup that is simple and comforting, made with ingredients like eggs, onions, herbs, and sometimes potatoes or flour. Here is a basic recipe:

Ingredients:

- 2 large onions (thinly sliced)
- 3 tablespoons vegetable oil or butter
- 2 tablespoons dried fenugreek leaves (shambalileh)
- 1 teaspoon turmeric
- 3-4 large eggs
- 2 tablespoons flour (optional for a thicker soup)
- 3-4 cups water (or vegetable/chicken broth)
- 2 medium potatoes (peeled and cubed, optional)
- Salt and pepper to taste
- 1-2 tablespoons vinegar (optional)
- Dried mint or fresh curly parsley for garnish

Instructions:

1. **Sauté the onions:** In a large pot, heat the oil or butter over medium heat. Add the sliced onions and cook until golden brown and caramelized, about 10-15 minutes. Stir frequently to avoid burning.
2. **Add spices:** Add the turmeric and dried fenugreek leaves to the onions, stirring well. Let the spices cook for about 2 minutes to release their aroma.
3. **Add water/broth:** Pour in the water or broth and bring the mixture to a boil. If you're using potatoes, add them now and cook until tender (about 10-15 minutes).
4. **Thicken the soup (optional):** If you want the soup to have a thicker consistency, dissolve the flour in a bit of cold water to create a smooth paste, then stir it into the soup.

5. **Cook the eggs:** Crack the eggs into the boiling soup one by one, stirring gently to break them up into the soup (like egg drop soup) or leave them whole for poached eggs. Cook until the eggs are set, about 5 minutes.
6. **Season and serve:** Add salt, pepper, and vinegar to taste. The vinegar gives a nice tang, but it's optional. Serve hot, garnished with dried mint or fresh curly parsley.

Variations:

Herbs: Fresh curly parsley can be added along with fenugreek for extra flavor.

Thickened Ashkaneh: My dad used flour for a richer texture.

Sponge Cake in the Time of War

When I walk into an American supermarket,
I always pass the sponge cake,
its fluffy surface a stark reminder
of promises made in the shadows of war.
I have never surrendered to it, nor shall I.
As a child, amidst the chaos,
my mother attempted a sponge cake,
her heart kneaded into the batter,
but it was the height of bombing season,
the kitchen shrouded in darkness,
illuminated only by the tremor of a gas lamp,
flickering, echoing London in ruins
during the Second World War.
By the door, a bundle of survival waited—
a bag heavy with desperation,
and baby formula for my newborn brother,
bought on the black market.
I longed for the sponge cake,
the sugar-dusted veil of my mother's promise,
but supper, an altar of fried onions,
soaked in boiled water,
dry bread crumbling,
eggs that bore the stench of the unholy.
Warplanes hovered like vulture shadows.
Our windows, fortified with tape,
heavy curtains draped like funeral veils,
offered little comfort.
No rescue stations,
no trains out of Tehran,
no flights to freedom.

Cars cloaked in darkness,
their lights painted blue to hide
from the eyes of a restless night.
We shared our fate with the cockroaches,
bound by fate, together maneuvering
the ruins of conflict.

Quince Jam

Mother's hands, dyed with love's ink,
stirred the pot of quince, saffron threads,
sharp, orange-gold, like secrets stirred in.
The glass jars lined the counter,
a row of silent soldiers at attention,
their smooth weight on the tongue—
a nostalgia that lives between the teeth,
a sweetness that mends words,
trust resewn in the tender pulp of fruit.
She would whisper about the cardamom—
cardamom added too early or too late—
how it shifted the color, like seasons in war,
or the ambush of lives fractured by shattered glass.
The fruit swelled, split open under heat,
its bruises spreading like news of the dead.
The wounded quince, doubling its bruises,
pours over me like an eternal drumbeat,
the impression of her voice lingering,
as if to revoke the war-ambushed mornings,
to reclaim peace with a jar of quince jam,
hands that cradled me when the bombs
dropped too close, when the windows shattered.
She could not keep the glass from breaking,
but she could make quince jam—
and even when the cardamom came too late,
it still found its way in,
like love in the aftermath of war.

Quince Jam Recipe

Ingredients:

- A couple of large quince (peel them, take out the cores, and chop them nicely)
- 4 cups of sugar (a little more or less, depending on how sweet you like it. You can also use agave if you prefer)
- 5-6 cups of water (enough to cover the quince)
- 1 tablespoon lemon juice (this keeps the sugar from getting hard)
- A small piece of cinnamon stick
- A dash of rose water (optional, but adds a wonderful fragrance)
- A couple of cardamoms (whole)

Instructions:

1. First things first, **peel and core your quinces**. Then chop them into pieces–not too big, not too small. Even pieces help them cook just right.
2. In a big pot, **put the chopped quinces** and enough water to cover them. Turn on the heat and bring it to a boil. Once it is bubbling away, lower the heat and let it simmer gently until the quinces soften. Add cardamoms and cinnamon stick. This takes about 30 to 40 minutes–be patient.
3. **Now, add your sugar**. Stir it gently, and you will see it dissolve into a lovely syrup. Do not forget to add the lemon juice, too–it helps the jam stay smooth and fresh.
4. **Let it cook slowly**. Keep the heat low and stir every now and then. You will notice the quince changes color–it might turn pink or even red, depending on the quince. Keep cooking until the jam thickens–this can take another 45 minutes to an hour. Do not rush it.

5. If you are feeling fancy, drop in that **cinnamon stick** for a bit of warmth, or a splash of rose water near the end for a beautiful scent.
6. **Here is how I check if it is ready**: take a spoonful and put it on a cold plate. Let it sit for a minute, then push it with your finger. If it wrinkles, it is done. If not, let it cook a bit longer.
7. Once it is ready, **turn off the heat** and let the jam cool just a little. Spoon it into clean jars while it is still warm. Seal them up and let them cool before you tuck them away.

A Jazz Echo of Alice Coltrane

Our eyes are wide like saucers,
hearts thumping after the bombings have ended,
a jazz echo of Alice Coltrane,
a drumbeat—
we need to breathe,
to dance as if tomorrow arrives,
and we will live to say we survived
without the guilt in the air like a thief.
Will the planes return?
Will we become nothing before we are this,
alive, moving together by melody,
familiar with this madness?
That sound, Alice's Universal Consciousness,
joy and agony tangled
in a world that forgets
how to hold its breath.
The notes scratch at our souls,
the fork stabbing at our throats
like a dentist's drill
against our teeth.
The haunting "what ifs" linger in our steps.

Grilling Fish: A Wartime Cuisine

It was a wedding—my uncle's, to be precise.
He had returned from Texas, where he had studied,
And now, he was getting married.
The wedding was small,
Just family and a few friends.
Because it was war,
My father, an artisan of flavor,
Carved two holes in the fertile earth,
Lined them with sturdy limbs of fruit trees;
Poison lurked in the wild—only fruit trees, he said.
Flames held close,
Muffled beneath the soil,
Kept from rising too high.
Nothing was as it could have been—
It was war.
The bride's white dress and veil
Might have been bloodied if rockets struck.
The fish, bare and unadorned—
No time for lavish marinades—
Placed on the grill,
Wore the essence of cherries,
Sour oranges, or naranj, as it is called in Iran.
Walnuts nestled within;
Fresh vegetables cradled in the fish's belly.
Pomegranate molasses wept,
Dripping sweetness into mouths—
A taste of paradise,
Even amid the ravages of war.

Grilled Fish on Fruit Branches

Ingredients:

- Whole fish (like trout) or fish fillets
- 2 tbsp olive oil
- Juice of 1 lemon
- Salt and pepper
- Clean branches from non-toxic fruit trees
  (apple, cherry, peach)

Instructions:

1. **Marinate fish:** Mix olive oil, lemon juice, salt, and pepper. Marinate the fish for 30 minutes.
2. **Prepare branches:** Select fresh, clean branches, about 2-3 feet long, and remove leaves and bark.
3. **Build fire:** Create a campfire or grill, allowing it to burn down to glowing coals.
4. **Skewer fish:** Run a branch through whole fish or place fillets on flat branches.
5. **Grill:** Cook over the fire for 10-15 minutes per side until flaky.
6. **Serve:** Carefully remove the fish and enjoy.

Soup for the Soul

My uncle—my mother's brother—
married and moved down the street,
a few cracked sidewalks away.
Their home, identical to ours,
had two floors and a garden,
but, their kitchen had windows.
When the air raid siren blared,
they rushed to our house in pajamas;
so if rockets hit us,
we would die together.
Perhaps it was the years of friendship,
and his time living with us after returning from the States,
that bound him to us.
It seemed logical to die together,
blood running as one.
One night, under flickering gaslight,
he made us soup.
Dense and white,
I never learned its name,
but it had a base of potatoes, onions, milk,
butter heavy as death's cold thumb,
seasoned with salt, pepper, and chopped spinach.
Now, when the cold winds claw
at the windows,
I hunger for that soup,
the warmth creeping up from the belly
while death sat patient at the door.
He is gone now, consumed by cancer,
and no one is left
to tell me what that soup was called.

Chilly Day Comfort Soup

Ingredients:

- 4 medium potatoes, peeled and diced
- 2 medium onions, chopped
- 4 cups whole milk (purchased on the black market)
- ¼ cup unsalted butter
- 1 teaspoon salt (adjust to taste)
- ½ teaspoon black pepper (adjust to taste)
- 2 cups fresh spinach, chopped (brought from Varamin, a small town outside Tehran)

Instructions:

1. **Prepare the vegetables:**
   - In a large pot, melt the butter over medium heat.
   - Add the chopped onions and sauté until they become translucent, about 5-7 minutes.
2. **Cook the potatoes:**
   - Add the diced potatoes to the pot and stir well to combine with the onions.
   - Cook for another 5 minutes, allowing the potatoes to absorb some of the butter and flavour.
3. **Add milk and simmer**
   - Pour in the whole milk and bring the mixture to a gentle simmer.
   - Reduce the heat to low and cover the pot. Let it simmer for about 20 minutes or until the potatoes are tender.
4. **Season the soup:**
   - Once the potatoes are cooked, add salt and pepper to taste.
   - Using a potato masher or immersion blender, mash or blend the soup until it reaches your desired consistency (smooth or slightly chunky).

5. **Incorporate spinach:**
    - Stir in the chopped spinach and cook for an additional 5 minutes or until wilted and tender.
6. **Serve:**
    - Ladle the soup into bowls and enjoy while hot, allowing the warmth to comfort you on a chilly day.

Notes:

This soup is perfect for cold weather, providing a sense of warmth and comfort.

Cooking to Bohemian Rhapsody

There was a recipe pinned to the board
of our windowless kitchen,
my father's gentle way of spinning tales
in the darkness and the war's weary embrace.
Blackouts cloaked the stars like heavy curtains,
and instead of bombs, we listened to Queen,
singing along to 'Bohemian Rhapsody,' echoing 'Bismillah'
as bombs fell, dropped by Muslims
on a country mostly Muslim.

With each rocket fired, every bomb tolling,
the word on everyone's lips was "Bismillah."
But Dad crafted his art of cooking, and each bite
was a careful measure, a recipe for survival,
stitched from remnants.
Outside, jasmine blooms sweetly
against the ash and soot of yesterday,
the rubble crumbling beneath our feet,
for every moment we held sacred—
each fleeting heartbeat intense,
unintelligible whispers of the past.
Yet we do not fade.
We unearth hope,
as life brings light and food brings feast,
rising above the ground.
Bismillah.

Chicken: A Rationed Recipe

There was a recipe pinned on the board on our kitchen wall. It was my dad's way of using humor in the time of war and blackouts.

Ingredients:

- 2 chicken breasts (sourced from local farms, representing resilience)
- A drizzle of olive oil (liquid gold, reminiscent of sunset)
- A dash of sea salt (to taste, whispering of ocean waves)
- Fresh herbs (dill and curly parsley, finely chopped like morning dew)
- 1 lemon (sliced thin, bright as a summer day)
- 3 cloves of garlic (minced, sharp as a sea breeze)
- A sprinkle of black pepper (like the night sky's specks)

Instructions:

Prepare the canvas:

1. Start with a clean, flat surface (as tranquil as a still sea).
2. Gently place the chicken breasts on the board, appreciating their humble origin.

Infuse the flavor:

1. Drizzle olive oil over the chicken, enveloping it in warmth.
2. Sprinkle with sea salt, letting it dance on the surface, a reminder of the ocean's embrace.
3. Add minced garlic, filling the air with its rich aroma, reminiscent of home cooking during uncertain times.

Herb tapestry:

1. Scatter fresh herbs, creating a vibrant green blanket, bringing the spirit of nature to life, even in rationed times.

Citrus burst:

1. Layer lemon slices on top, like sunlit clouds, their juice promising brightness and joy in each bite, a taste of hope amid hardship.

Cooking process:

1. Heat a skillet until it shimmers (like sunlit waves).
2. Carefully place the chicken in, letting it sizzle and sing.
3. Cook for about 6-7 minutes per side until golden brown, flipping gently, cherishing it as a treasured meal in times of scarcity.

Presenting the dish:

1. Transfer to a plate, bright and enticing, a small victory on the table.
2. Garnish with remaining herbs for a final touch of green, symbolizing resilience.
3. Serve alongside roasted vegetables or a crisp salad, celebrating the simple pleasures found in shared meals.

The feast:

1. Gather around the table, filled with friends and laughter, sharing stories of survival and hope.
2. Enjoy the fruits of your labor, each bite a reminder of resilience, community, and the human spirit's endurance amid war and rationing.

Notes:

You may die by rockets or bombs, but you have to eat in case you survive and in case tomorrow there are no chickens around.

Pair with a crisp white wine (a toast to enduring spirits), though wine is nowhere to be found unless it is bought in hiding because the totalitarian regime forbids it.

Let the flavors mingle like currents in the deep.

Savor the moment, for this dish, born from adversity, is now complete.

Koloocheh

As a child, I turned away from Koloocheh,
the Persian cookie dense with walnuts,
their stubborn bulk pushing against sweetness,
as if they did not belong.
Maybe it was the heft of them,
the way they crowded my tongue,
unwelcome, uninvited.
But now, when I step into any Persian store in America,
I reach for them with a kind of hunger,
each bite a return,
a small remembering.
Memories without walnuts,
like pages left unwritten,
or a sky that refuses clouds.

Koloocheh Zaboli

Koloocheh is a pastry often filled with dates, cinnamon, or walnuts. This recipe is from Iran's southeastern province. One spring, during the Persian New Year, bombs hit Tehran hard, and schools were closed. We traveled to Zabol in Baluchistan, where I watched women make koloocheh with dates and flour, baking it in a clay oven. You can use a regular oven for this recipe.

Ingredients:

- Flour: 1½ cups
- Solid oil (shortening): ⅓ cup
- Sugar: 1 tablespoon
- Baking powder: 1 teaspoon
- Milk: 6 heaping tablespoons
- Salt: ½ teaspoon
- Black seeds (Nigella seeds): 1 teaspoon
- Anise or fennel seeds: 1 teaspoon
- Cumin: ½ teaspoon
- Dates: 12

Instructions:

1. Place the oil and flour in a bowl and mix thoroughly until the flour absorbs the oil. *No mixer is needed; traditionally, the women did this by hand, but you can also use a spoon if you prefer.*
2. Add the baking powder, salt, and sugar to the bowl, then gradually mix in the milk.
3. Add the black seeds (*Nigella sativa*, a medicinal plant from the Ranunculaceae family, also known as black cumin due to its cumin-like appearance), anise and cumin. Mix well. The dough might feel sticky initially, but as you knead, the milk will absorb fully into the mixture.

4. Knead the dough thoroughly for about 5 minutes. This step will help the koloocheh hold its shape better when baked.
5. Peel the dates, remove the pits, and place them in a pan with a bit of oil over low heat for about 5 minutes until softened.
6. Divide the dough into portions, each roughly the size of two walnuts.
7. To form the koloocheh, you can use various folding methods. Add a bit of date paste to each piece of dough, fold it closed, and seal.
8. Another option is to cut the dough with a round cutter, place date paste in the center, fold it into a triangle, add a decorative pattern on top, and bake until done.

Boil the Eggs Until Firm, Potatoes Tender in Their Bath

The rockets fell like rain,
each strike nearer,
driving us to the back of a rusted truck—
me, my mother,
the youngest of my two brothers.
The other,
gone with my father across borders,
as we planned our escape,
Tehran shrinking in the rearview of war.
Nine hundred kilometers of dust-choked road,
the heat pressing down.
We had no feast, just boiled eggs,
potato salad, wrapped in cloth—
the taste of survival,
held between cracked fingers,
salted with sweat and silence.
Our world boiled down to this:
eggs, potatoes, whispers of escape,
the weight of kilometers.
Boil the eggs until firm, potatoes tender in their bath.
Once cooled, strip bare of skin and shell,
lay them gently on the kitchen counter.
A quarter cup of cream—
mayonnaise or Greek yogurt—
whispers a lighter touch.
One spoon of mustard (if you wish),
olive oil, lemon's tart kiss,
salt and pepper, dash to taste.
Chop green onions, chives like dreams,
Parsley, pickles for that extra bite.

Toss them into the waiting bowl—
potatoes cubed, eggs crumbled soft.
Together, they wait for what is to come.
Pour the dressing slow,
folding the flavors,
letting them grow.
Slice bread, pack for the road.

Egg Potato Salad Recipe

Ingredients:

Salad:

- 4 medium potatoes (peeled and diced)
- 4 hard-boiled eggs (chopped)
- 1 cup celery (finely chopped)
- ½ cup red onion (finely chopped)
- ½ cup dill pickles (optional, diced)

Dressing:

1 cup mayonnaise
1 tbsp Dijon mustard
1 tbsp apple cider vinegar (or lemon juice)
Salt and pepper (to taste)
1 tsp garlic powder (optional)
Fresh dill or curly parsley (optional for garnish)

Instructions:

1. **Cook potatoes:** Boil diced potatoes in salted water until tender (10-15 mins). Drain and cool.
2. **Prepare eggs:** Hard-boil the eggs, cool, peel, and chop.
3. **Make dressing:** Whisk together mayonnaise, Dijon mustard, vinegar, garlic powder (if using), salt, and pepper.
4. **Combine:** In a large bowl, mix cooled potatoes, chopped eggs, celery, red onion, and pickles. Pour dressing over and gently toss.
5. **Chill:** Refrigerate for at least 1 hour. Adjust seasoning before serving, and garnish with dill or curly parsley if desired.

I Press Walnuts into the Scars of War

I scatter walnuts like seeds—
into salads, over bread smeared with feta,
stirred into chicken with pomegranate molasses, saffron, and honey
each bite, a bridge back to something
I did not realize I had lost.

I press walnuts into the scars of war,
let their earthy taste fill the cracks,
with something rich, something real.

And watch
as butterflies with broken wings
find their flutter again,
fragile but flying.

Each walnut, a piece of me returned.

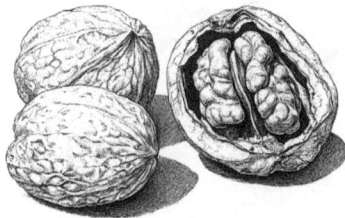

Feta, Walnut, and Mint Salad

Ingredients:

- 1 cup feta cheese (crumbled)
- ½ cup walnuts (toasted and chopped)
- 2 tablespoons dried mint
- Olive oil (optional, for drizzling)
- Salt and pepper (to taste)

Instructions:

1. **Combine ingredients:** In a bowl, mix the crumbled feta, chopped walnuts, and dried mint.
2. **Season:** Add salt and pepper to taste. Drizzle with olive oil if desired.
3. **Serve:** Toss gently to combine and enjoy.

Desert Garden

In the home garden, the persimmon tree stood tall,
Branches heavy with promise, ripe skins twisting.
Each bite a burst.
In the windowless kitchen,
Fanning in and out,
Turquoise earrings glimmer,
As grandmother's long, silky hair flows like rain.
Her green eyes bright, alive with the storm,
Walking with umbrellas like drunken sailors.
Defying taxis, she claimed the world with each step,
Strolling an hour from her home to ours.
Good with plants, she nurtured life,
Creating Persian feasts, sholehzard in the making,
Even when rice was rationed—
This desert was hers.
Mixing persimmon fruits with water, skin and all,
Letting it cool in the fridge like gelatin,
Sprinkling cinnamon on top.
This was a substitute for saffron-cooked rice,
Heavy with sugar and covered in cinnamon for dessert.
War inspired its own creativity,
In the absence and lack of ingredients.

Sholehzard

This is a classic Persian saffron rice pudding. Here is a simple recipe to make at home:

Ingredients:

- 1 cup basmati rice
- 4 cups of water
- 1 cup sugar (adjust to taste)
- ½ cup of rose water
- ¼ teaspoon ground saffron (or a few saffron threads soaked in 2 tablespoons of hot water)
- ¼ cup slivered almonds (for garnish)
- ¼ cup chopped pistachios (for garnish)
- Cinnamon powder (for garnish)

Instructions:

1. **Rinse the rice:** Wash the basmati rice under cold water until the water runs clear to eliminate excess starch. Soak the rice in water for 1-2 hours, then drain.
2. **Cook the rice:** In a large pot, bring 4 cups of water to a boil. Add the soaked and drained rice, then lower the heat to medium. Cook until the rice is tender and fully cooked (about 15-20 minutes).
3. **Mash the rice:** After cooking, turn off the heat and mash the rice with a fork or potato masher until it achieves a creamy texture.
4. **Add sugar and saffron:** Incorporate the sugar, rose water, and saffron (including the soaking water if using threads). Stir thoroughly until the sugar is fully dissolved.
5. **Simmer:** Return the pot to low heat and allow it to simmer for about 10-15 minutes, stirring occasionally to prevent sticking. The mixture should thicken to a pudding-like consistency.

6. **Cool down:** Remove the pot from heat and let it cool slightly. Transfer the sholezard to serving dishes or a large platter.
7. **Garnish:** Once it reaches room temperature, top with slivered almonds, chopped pistachios, and a sprinkle of cinnamon.
8. **Chill:** For the best flavor, cover and refrigerate the sholezard for a few hours before serving. It can be enjoyed chilled or at room temperature.

Raw Vegan Sholehzard

This is a raw vegan sholehzard that my family made during the war because sugar and rice were rationed. Use a blender with water, a couple of rinsed persimmons, and some saffron.
Pour it into small bowls and let it cool. Add cinnamon powder and blanched almonds on top, then place it in the fridge before serving.

Breakfasting in the Time of War

A dreary chorus of peasants,
Carrots sliced like whispers,
Their orange faces submerged in gloom
My father stirs the lentils—
In the frost-draped dawn, the kitchen buzzes,

A spoonful of butter,
A glimmer of gold,
Warmed by the electric ache of
Stevie Nicks' haunting refrain,
A song that weaves through the crumbling air.

Cereal and milk, ghosts on the black market,
Bartered dreams among the rubble,
While outside, the sky weeps,
Snow cloaks the chaos,
And bombs fall like forgotten thoughts,
Echoing a second world war,
A stark reminder of our fragile meal.

Yet here, in this frail sanctuary,
Lentils boil, thick and dark,
A flicker of warmth against the cold.
Each spoonful a tether to life.

Adasi (lentils) Soup Recipe

Ingredients:

- 1 cup lentils (green or brown)
- 1 medium onion, finely chopped
- 2-3 cloves garlic, minced
- 1 medium tomato, chopped (optional)
- 1 teaspoon turmeric powder
- 1 teaspoon cumin powder
- Salt and pepper, to taste
- 2 tablespoons oil (vegetable or olive)
- 4 cups water or vegetable broth
- Fresh herbs (such as curly parsley or cilantro) for garnish
- 1 tablespoon lemon or lime juice

Instructions:

1. **Rinse the lentils:**
   - Rinse the lentils under cold water until the water runs clear to remove any impurities.
2. **Cook the lentils:**
   - In a pot, combine the rinsed lentils and 4 cups of water or broth. Bring to a boil, then reduce the heat to low and let simmer for about 20-25 minutes, or until the lentils are tender but not mushy.
3. **Sauté the onions and garlic:**
   - In a separate pan, heat the oil over medium heat. Add the chopped onions and sauté until they turn translucent, about 5-7 minutes.
   - Add the minced garlic and sauté for an additional minute until fragrant.
4. **Add spices:**
   - Stir in the turmeric, cumin, salt, and pepper. Cook for 1-2 minutes to toast the spices.

5. **Combine ingredients:**
   - Add the cooked lentils to the onion and spice mixture. If using, incorporate the chopped tomatoes and stir well to combine.
6. **Simmer:**
   - Let it simmer for an additional 10-15 minutes to meld the flavors.
7. **Serve:**
   - Serve hot. Add lemon or lime juice. You can garnish the dish with fresh herbs.

Tips:
- Adjust the spices to your liking.
- Adasi is often served with Persian bread.
- Consider adding diced potatoes or carrots for extra flavor and texture.

In Between the Bombings

In the quiet spaces between the bombings, my father—still in Iran—
would gather my brothers and me, a trio of restless spirits,
and drive us out to parks lined with old plane trees.
He would scoop out the baguettes, and when I asked why,
his eyes would soften, a gentle shield against worry,
"Just to spare you from bellyaches."
Then he filled each hollow with chopped curly parsley,
red onions, pickles, slices of ripe tomatoes, and cuts of bologna.
Water sloshed in the Coleman jug in back—just in case—
though every park had fountains,
bubbling like clear laughter, always enough.
On those weekly trips, war softened,
became the echo of someone else's life,
and we were just kids, darting through dappled shade,
biting into our sandwiches, fresh bread and green life,
while my father watched us, still as a tree, inhaling our joy.

Hearty Baguette Sandwich Recipe

Ingredients:

- 1 large baguette
- 1 cup fresh curly parsley, chopped
- 1 small red onion, finely diced
- 1 cup pickles, sliced (no sweet pickles)
- 2 ripe tomatoes, sliced
- 8 oz bologna (or your favorite deli meat), sliced
- Salt and pepper to taste
- Optional: mayonnaise or mustard for spreading

Instructions:

1. **Prepare the baguette:**
   - If you want a warm sandwich, preheat your oven to 350°F (175°C).
   - Slice the baguette in half lengthwise, and carefully scoop out some of the soft interior to create space for the filling. Place it in the oven for a few minutes.
2. **Mix the filling:**
   - In a bowl, combine the chopped curly parsley, diced red onion, sliced pickles, and tomato slices. Toss gently to mix.
   - Season with salt and pepper to your taste.
3. **Assemble the sandwich:**
   - If you like, spread a thin layer of mayonnaise or mustard inside the hollowed baguette.
   - Layer the bologna slices inside, followed by the curly parsley mixture.
4. **Close and serve:**
   - Reassemble the baguette halves. If you warm it, place it in the oven for about 5-10 minutes until slightly crispy.
   - Slice it into individual portions and enjoy your hearty sandwich.

Our Lives, Our Breaths, Our Blood

After camping, we would return from the Caspian Sea,
sometimes sneaking rice—those tiny grains of rebellion—
against a regime that thought they could hoard
our lives, our breaths, our blood, all of it.
As if we were just bodies,
you know, like living corpses,
trudging through the heat.
My father, with a life in disguise,
perceived the world through a historian's eyes,
sharp as a blade, trained for war,
finding the crevices of the car,
crannies where hope was stored,
hidden treasures of grain.
We would curl up in the back,
my brothers and I,
sick on too many cherries,
the sting of raw garlic lingering.
The sun's weight pressing down,
laughter tangled with our fights for space,
while guards loomed outside like wolves,
heavy guns resting against their sides,
interrogating us with their eyes.
We feigned innocence,
an act draped in pain,
though sometimes the pain was real—
too many cherries bubbling inside.
Oh, those bike rides on the beach,
the salt in our hair,
a fleeting taste of freedom
before we faced the drive back
to the heart of the city,
where cockroaches scuttled and the bombs kept coming.
Whilst in that wisp, we were winning—
wielding precious rice bags tucked beneath us.

Kateh

This is a traditional Persian rice dish known for its simplicity and rich flavor. Here is a basic recipe for cooking Kateh:

Ingredients:

- 2 cups basmati rice
- 4 cups water (or adjust as needed)
- 2-3 tablespoons vegetable oil or butter
- Salt, to taste
- Optional: saffron or herbs

Instructions:

1. **Rinse the rice:**
   - Place the basmati rice in a bowl and rinse it under cold water until the water is clear. This helps remove excess starch and prevents the rice from becoming sticky. Soak the rinsed rice in water for about 30 minutes, then drain.
2. **Cook:**
   - In a large pot, add 4 cups of water and salt to taste. Bring water to a boil.
3. **Incorporate the rice:**
   - Once the water is boiling, add the drained rice. Stir gently to combine and allow it to return to a boil.
4. **Simmer:**
   - After it boils again, reduce the heat to low and cover the pot with a tight-fitting lid. Let it simmer for about 25-30 minutes, trying not to lift the lid during this time to ensure even cooking.
5. **Check for doneness:**
   - After 25-30 minutes, check the rice. It should be tender, and the water should have been absorbed. If needed, add a little more water and cook for a few more minutes.

6. **Fluff and serve:**
   - Once the rice is cooked, fluff it gently with a fork to separate the grains. Serve it hot alongside your choice of dishes, such as grilled meats, stews, or vegetables.

Tips
- For extra flavor, consider adding saffron threads soaked in a bit of warm water to the rice during the last few minutes of cooking.
- You can also mix in herbs like dry dill.

Fractured

Straddling the streets we knew, but no longer,
Bodies broken, broken bodies—
Everything broken, doors and windows
Cars creaking under the weight.
Human lives lost—
The most extreme, expiring sequences,
Seasons turning east, then north, then south,
Left, not right—
Not right, where once
Was now and touch.
Swelling eyes, like fish gasping out of water,
Water spilled, flooding the cracks.
We trace the outlines of what was,
War was war was war was war.

In the Heart of the Falling City

Innocence bends,
Sadness quenches,
Alliances forged.
Glass leaves flutter and lapse.
Witness as time gently wraps
Nina Simone,
modern love dancing—
David Bowie's orange
in the back of an ambulance,
leaving one town for the next,
bombs dropping behind us.
War is real.
Justice calls from the folds
in the heart of the falling city,
and dreams that cease to last.

Garden Fresh Watermelon Bowl

The recipe for Persian watermelon, feta cheese, and bread.

Ingredients:

- Watermelon: 4 cups, cubed (approximately half a medium watermelon)
- Feta cheese: 1 cup, crumbled (you can use traditional feta or a softer variety)
- Fresh mint: ¼ cup, chopped (basil can be used as an alternative)
- Bread: 4 slices of your choice (pita, lavash, or sourdough work well)

Instructions:

1. **Prepare the watermelon**:
   - Cut the cold watermelon into bite-sized cubes and place them in a large mixing bowl.
2. **Combine feta and mint**:
   - Add the crumbled feta cheese and chopped fresh mint to the watermelon. Gently toss the ingredients together, taking care not to mash the feta.
3. **Prepare the bread**:
   - If you are using pita or lavash, cut it into triangles.
4. **Serve**:
   - Arrange the watermelon and feta salad on a platter and serve alongside the bread.

Aftermath

Across the dark, silence roamed,
Hands reaching into the air—
A prayer or a curse, anger, helplessness;
Terror trickled like the dregs of a coffee cup,
Telling the tale of tangled traces.

Spoon and Shrapnel

Spoon and shrapnel haunt like breath.
Peach skies thin above peach trees
in quiet dust where bombs once tore—
rockets no longer screech through.
Bruised red bursts of pomegranate's womb,
the dead reeling forth from tomb to tomb,
as warm air wraps new life—
blind as bone, bountiful.

OTHER POETRY TITLES FROM DARAJA PRESS

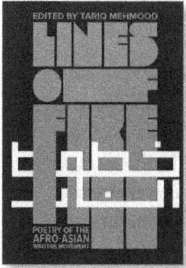

COMING SOON
Lines of Fire • Edited by Tariq Mehmood

This collection of poems features voices that were persecuted for the power of their words. The poetry cries out against the injustices and brutality of the colonial powers of their time, raging against tyranny and the festering wounds of racism, especially in Palestine. Many of the writers of the Afro-Asian Writers Movement faced torture, imprisonment, exile, and even death, but their words continue to call for a just world.

ISBN 978-1-990263-45-3

Night Settles Upon the City • Omar Sabbagh

Written with urgency out of a war-time Beirut, this poetry collection registers the griefs and the heroism of the Lebanese, under siege yet again. Sabbagh lends his lyrical voice here, to give a voice to the voiceless, trying to find some harmonic sense out of catastrophe. This book will compel readers, both Lebanese and those with any kind of human heart.

ISBN 978-1-998309-33-7 • 82 pages • $16.00

Palestine Wail • Yahya Lababidi

Yahya Lababidi reminds us that religion is not politics, Judaism is not Zionism, and to criticize the immoral, illegal actions of Israel is not antisemitism — especially since, as an Arab, Lababidi is a Semite, himself Using both poetry and prose, Lababidi reflects on how we are neither our corrupt governments, nor our compromised media. Rather, we are partners in humanity, members of one human family.

ISBN 978-1-998309-11-5 • 116 pages • $18.00

Elsewhereness • S Bahodze

The book is a literary project with extra-literary objectives and implications. The texts combine various original writing styles to provoke the reader's creative imagination and make auratic social space attainable. For realizing its main goal, through its creative aesthetics, the book debases normalized forms of social violence, exclusionism, and tribalism. It is meant to be universally relatable by an average reader regardless of her perceived and proclaimed identities.

ISBN 978-1-998309-28-3 • 60 pages • $9.00

Order from **darajapress.com** or **zandgraphics.com**
Prices in U.S. dollars

Daraja Press

MORE POETRY TITLES FROM DARAJA PRESS

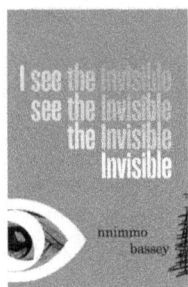

I See the Invisible • Nnimmo Bassey

I never thought I would write another volume of poetry after the last, I will not Dance to Your Beat *(2011). The reason was that my previous volumes were reactive to the circumstances of the times. So ehat you have in your hands, or on your screens, is a compilation that is largely more meditative than the previous collections. There are moments of reflection on the colonial and neoliberal foundations that permit a willful disconnection from nature and the resultant destructive extractivism.* – Nnimmo Bassey

ISBN 978-1-990263-89-7 • 148 pages • $20

Love After Babel • Chandramohan S

Winner of the Nicolás Cristóbal Guillén Batista Outstanding Book Award from the Caribbean Philosophical Association

Love after Babel *deals with themes such as caste, the resistance of Dalit people, Dalit literature, islamophobia and other political themes, in almost one hundred poems. The introduction is by Suraj Yengde, award-winning scholar and activist from India.*

ISBN 978-1-988832-37-1 • 110 pages • $15.30

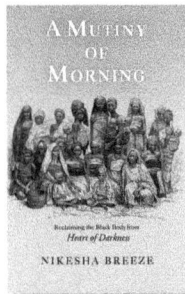

A Mutiny of Morning • Nikesha Breeze

Nikesha Breeze has taken words from Joseph Conrad's *Heart of Darkness* and forced them to leave his colonized mind in a radical, surgical, and unapologetic Black appropriation. The resulting poems are sizzling purifications, violent restorations of integrity, pain, wound, bewilderment, rage, and sometimes luminous generosity.

ISBN 978-1-990263-35-42 • 100 pages • $30

Love Pandemic • Salimah Valiani

These poems were largely written during the first wave of the COVID-19 pandemic. The last poem in the collection was written at the start of the second wave in Africa. Most were circulated through Whatsapp voice notes, an intimate way of keeping distance while reaching out to touch.

ISBN 978-1-990263-53-8 • 32 pages • $10

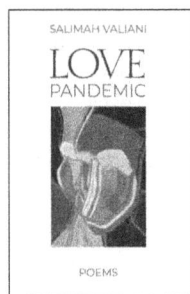

Daraja Press

Order from **darajapress.com** or **zandgraphics.com**
Prices in U.S. dollars

www.ingramcontent.com/pod-product-compliance
Lightning Source LLC
Chambersburg PA
CBHW071953100426
42736CB00043B/3183